The Partial CAPO

The Basics, Tips, Tricks, and More

by Randall Williams

PLAYBACK➕
Speed Pitch Balance Loop

To access audio visit:
www.halleonard.com/mylibrary

3612-0378-6268-5273

ISBN: 978-1-4234-2136-8

HAL•LEONARD®
7777 W. BLUEMOUND RD. P.O. BOX 13819 MILWAUKEE, WI 53213

Visit Hal Leonard Online at
www.halleonard.com

In Australia Contact:
Hal Leonard Australia Pty. Ltd.
4 Lentara Court
Cheltenham, Victoria, 3192 Australia
Email: ausadmin@halleonard.com

FOREWORD

by David Wilcox

So there's finally a map to this territory! Thanks, Randall. I've made my way through this wilderness for years without seeing the big picture.

I love how this book maps out lots of different ways of thinking about how to use cut capos. There's something here for everyone, even if you've never tried open-string capos.

Give some of the easy techniques a try and I think you'll love the frontier of beautiful sounds that's waiting for you.

David Wilcox, September 2006
www.davidwilcox.com

CONTENTS

Audio recorded by Peter Stevens at Freedlight Sonics, St. Louis

INTRODUCTION

"The environment for wonder on the guitar is already mapped—
but this is a whole new universe."

- David Wilcox

A partial capo is nothing to be afraid of. It's just a tool, like a fingerpick or a slide. But a partial capo revolutionizes the way we approach the guitar. A partial capo is just like a regular capo—a little clamp that helps you change pitch easily—but it leaves some strings open.

In visual art, we speak of depth of field as it relates to perspective. The tiny mountains in a painting are far away; the immense trees are close to us. The image has a foreground and a background because of our understanding of depth of field. A partial capo creates this kind of depth of field on the guitar.

The roadmap for using partial capos is simple, but the variations are deeply complex. Capos have been around for a few hundred years, partial capos for only a few decades. By the time you finish this book, you'll have a good map, but the territory you find on your own may be uncharted. Enjoy your exploration and the discovery that comes with it.

Bon voyage!

A Word About Notation

There are two different notation possibilities for partial capos. In this book, chord charts are labeled in both the sounding key (top symbol) and the chord being voiced (bottom symbol in parentheses), just as you would with a full capo. Occasionally, the open strings used in conjunction with the partial capo may create a more complex harmony than the fingered chord. In these instances, the top symbol will reflect the full harmony in the sounding key, and the bottom symbol in parentheses will reflect the chord being voiced (or the one it most closely resembles). Strings marked with "o" are both open strings and strings that are open in relation to the capo.

In partial capo tablature, open strings are "o," with the capoed frets in bold. This is simply because it's common to play behind a partial capo (on the lower frets, behind where the capo is clamped). In the case of multiple capos where some transcribers might use different colored numbers, both bold and gray numbers will be used.

ABOUT THE AUTHOR

Randall Williams holds undergraduate and conservatory degrees in music. He's a classically trained baritone who specializes in teaching structure for the acoustic guitar through partial capo work and open tunings. More often than on the classical stage, Randall can be found performing on the international singer-songwriter circuit promoting his four CDs.

Listen to music and see teaching videos at Randall's online home, www.whereisrandall.com.

A Word About Capo Placement and Intonation

With any capo, it's important to clamp it parallel to the frets and as close to the fret as possible, like this:

The capo shouldn't get in the way of your hand, but if it does, you can move it back some. The main reason to clamp it close to the fret has to do with keeping the guitar in tune (see below).

This is going to be especially important when using more than one capo at a time.

Put the capo on without pushing the strings out of alignment like this:

When the capo pushes down on the strings, the bend required to clamp them can pull them slightly out of tune. Sometimes that can be too much, especially with light or extra light gauge strings, or if your strings are high off the fretboard (high action). If this happens, it's best to adjust your tuning *after* you place the capo.

Sometimes beginning guitarists will push strings out of alignment when they play by pushing too hard on some chords. It's important to watch yourself, and listen to make sure what you're playing sounds in tune.

The Roadmap: What a Capo Does

You can do two things with a capo: you can change **pitch**, or you can keep that pitch and change your chord **voicings**. The easiest way to approach partial capo work is through voicing changes. We'll get there in just a second, after we talk briefly about changing pitch. It helps to start thinking about both by using a full capo first. Before we get started though, let's tune up. Listen to *track 55* for tuning pitches.

Changing Pitch

If you play a D chord, then you hear a D chord. But if you play a D chord with a full capo on the second fret, then you hear an E chord. You're still fingering the same triangle-shaped chord in both cases, but with the capo on the second fret, you hear that chord one step higher. You've *raised* the pitch.

TRACK 1

The basic D major voicing—you hear D.

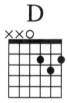

TRACK 2

The same D voicing, two frets up—you hear E.

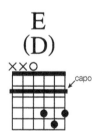

TRACK 3

If you continue to move the capo up the neck and play the same D chord, the pitch will keep moving up. You'll discover that the guitar sounds very different once you're playing it higher up. Listen to *track 3* for an example of this.

Changing Voicings

Changing voicings is a little more involved than just moving the capo up. Now we're moving the capo up, but changing the chord shapes we play so that we stay in the same key.

If you play an E chord without a capo, you hear E. If you move the capo up to the second fret but play a D chord, you still hear an E (like in the previous example). You can continue capoing higher up the neck, playing different voicings so you're still hearing E.

It works like this:

TRACK 4

Here's a D chord with the capo on fret 2. You hear E, even though you're playing a regular D chord.

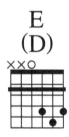

TRACK 5

Here's a C chord with the capo on the fourth fret. Notice that as you move the capo up, you move the chord voicing *down* — dropping from D to C. You're still hearing E.

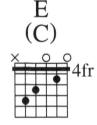

As you continue to take the capo up, the chord voicing keeps dropping down. We'll discuss exactly how this works later.

Here's an A chord with the capo on the seventh fret—just like an E barre chord, right? And you still hear E.

E
(A)

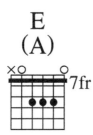

TRACK 7

You can even capo all the way up the neck at the ninth fret and play a G chord, and still hear E. Now the guitar sounds almost like a mandolin.

E
(G)

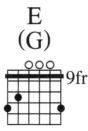

Changing the voicing like this works in any key—E is just the easiest one to understand, and it makes partial capo work easy, too.

Starting Off: The Drop "D" Capo

"Without partial capos, I'd have to carry nine guitars to each of my shows."

- Janis Ian

The "drop D" position is the place to start with partial capoing. On page 6 we saw that by voicing a D chord and moving the capo up two frets, you're actually hearing an E chord.

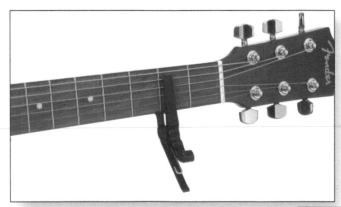

With the capo still on the second fret, remove the capo from the sixth (low E) string only. With standard clamp-style capos, you can do this by capoing from the bottom side of the neck and moving the capo down so it leaves the low string open.

Or you can buy a Drop "D" capo, which intentionally leaves that string unclamped. It's not a silly investment — there are good reasons to use the right capo for the job.

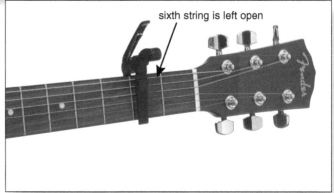

sixth string is left open

The D chord that you're voicing is raised two frets because of the capo — so you're actually hearing an E chord, right? And the low E string is open, which gives a nice, deep bass note.

TRACK 8

So now instead of playing only four strings in this standard capoed D chord...

E
(D)
×× ○

TRACK 9

E
(D)
○ ○ ○
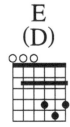

...you can play all six strings in this very rich-sounding D chord.

Some people think of this capo position as "drop D" because it sounds the same as drop D tuning (only a whole step higher). But this isn't drop D tuning. In drop D tuning, you tune the low E string to D. As a result, you have to change the fingerings in order to play chords that use the sixth string.

The good news is that with partial capos, the tuning doesn't change. So most often, you don't have to change fingerings. Let's look at how this works.

TRACK 10

In drop D tuning, the G chord looks like this:

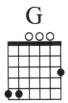

TRACK 11

But with the Drop "D" capo, the G chord hand position doesn't change.

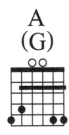

TRACK 12

One chord that *does* change is the Em—only because you need that low-string note for the chord. You can deal with this by fingering the low string on the same fret as the capo, like this:

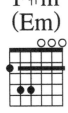

By no accident, all of these chords we're fingering are in the key of D. We'll be talking a lot more about keys later in the book, but for now let's lay out the chords in the key of D. Substituting a ♭VII chord for the traditional diminished vii, they are: D, Em, F♯m, G, A, Bm, and C. All of those chords work great with the Drop "D" capo in that position.

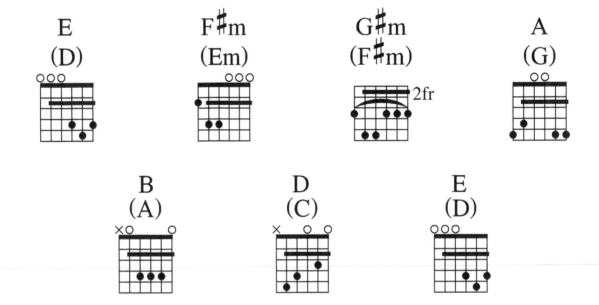

Listen to *track 13* to hear how some of these sound.

TRACK 13

Changing Voicings

On page 8, we saw that we could stay in the same key by raising the capo and playing different chord **voicings**. That's the best roadmap for approaching partial capos. With the capo on the second fret, we played in the key of D. Now, if we move the capo up to the fourth fret, we can voice chords in the key of C.

TRACK 14

Here's a C chord with the Drop "D" capo on fret 4. Notice that as you move the capo up, you move the chord voicing *down*, dropping from D to C. But you're still hearing an E chord.

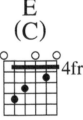

TRACK 15

The chords in the key of C (again substituting the ♭VII) are C, Dm, Em, F, G, Am, and B♭. Try playing those chords in this capo position, remembering that the low string is open, and you can use it when you like. This works particularly well for the C and F chords. Listen to *track 15*.

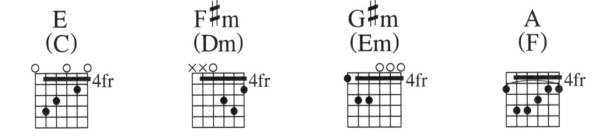

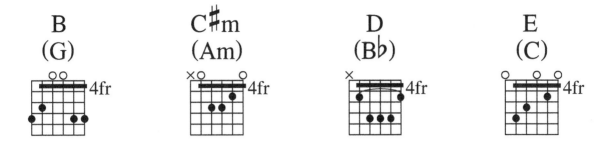

B
(G)

4fr

C#m
(Am)

4fr

D
(B♭)

4fr

E
(C)

4fr

TRACK 16

Here's an A chord with the Drop "D" capo on fret 7—just like a E barre chord, right? And you still hear E.

E
(A)

7fr

You can play any of these major or minor keys, and they work just fine. With the capo on the second fret, you can play in the key of D or D minor, and with the capo on the fourth fret you can play in C or C minor. You're probably less likely to choose C minor because it's full of barre chords. But here on the seventh fret, A minor is actually easier to negotiate than A major because there are fewer barres.

TRACK 17

Track 17 demonstrates these chords: Am, B♭, C, Dm, Em, E major, F, and G. They all work well in the key of Am, and the sixth-string drone gives a nice fullness to your sound when the rest of the strings are capoed up so high.

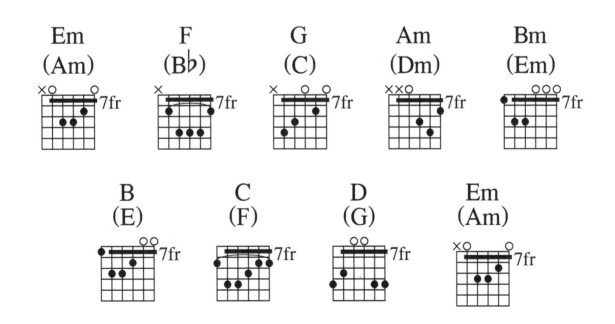

Em
(Am)

7fr

F
(B♭)

7fr

G
(C)

7fr

Am
(Dm)

7fr

Bm
(Em)

7fr

B
(E)

7fr

C
(F)

7fr

D
(G)

7fr

Em
(Am)

7fr

TRACK 18

You can even capo all the way up the neck at the ninth fret and play a G chord, and still hear E. Now the guitar sounds almost like a mandolin. You can also leave the sixth string open if you'd like to get a nice, full bass note.

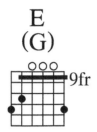

TRACK 19

In the key of G, you can play G, Am, Bm, C, D, Em, and F—and they all sound good. *Track 19* demonstrates. Remember that for Em, you need to finger the sixth string on the same fret as the capo.

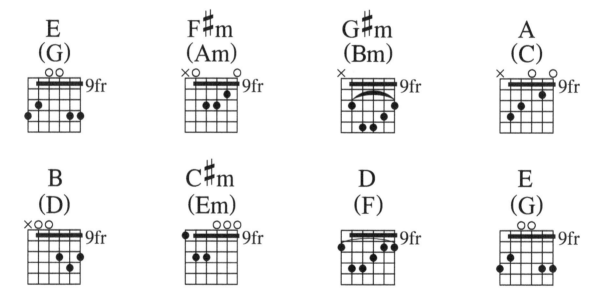

Partial Capos:
Not the Same as Open Tunings!

There's a tendency to think that using a partial capo is the equivalent of an open tuning. Partial capos will give you new sounds that can be similar to open tunings, but they're not the same. Here's why:

1. When you change tuning, you have to change your fingerings. Once tuned to DADGAD, for example, the same triangle-shaped D voicing that you're used to playing in standard tuning isn't going to sound the same at all.

2. When you play a voicing with no open strings, you don't hear the partial capo at all. The only time you hear the partial capo is when you take advantage of the sounds that the open strings create. Sometimes these sound like an open tuning, although the guitar is still tuned E–A–D–G–B–E.

That being said, partial capos make it easy for beginning guitarists and Grammy winners alike to get lots of new sounds from the guitar.

Color and Structure

The next crucial concept to understand is the difference between **color** and **structure**.

Using the Drop "D" capo on the second fret with the low E string open, you're making a **structural** decision, because the low note is a very important note in the chord. That means when using the open sixth string, you can't just play any chord; you need to play chords which sound good with that low E drone.

However, if you reverse the capo and leave the high E string open, it's a **color** decision. The chord isn't being fundamentally changed; you're just adding notes (color) to it.

TRACK 20

Here's how that works: With the Drop "D" capo on the second fret, fingering a C chord and leaving the low string open can sound a little muddy.

D/E
(C)

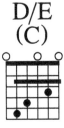

TRACK 21

But with the capo turned around and the high string open, that C chord sounds just fine.

Dadd9
(C)

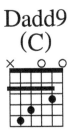

With the high string open, you can stumble upon lots of different chords that work in a number of positions. The roadmap of staying in the key of E is useful, but trial and error can be fun, too.

This structure/color distinction will become more important once you're dealing with more open strings; such is the case with the Short-Cut capo.

The Short-Cut Capo

The Short-Cut capo clamps down on three inner strings and leaves three outer strings open. In the standard position, this means that the sixth (low E) string is open, as are the two high strings (B and E.)

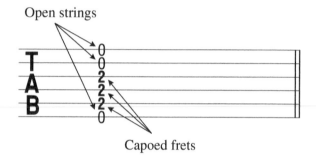

The Short-Cut is similar to the Drop "D" capo that we've already looked at, but it's slightly more comlicated. Used in the standard position, the Short-Cut offers **one structural choice** (the open sixth string), and **two color choices** (the open first and second strings).

Remember our roadmap for partial capo work—we'll stay in the key of E. As the capo moves up, we'll drop the chord voicing down so that we're still hearing E.

D Major

With the Short-Cut on the second fret, let's start by voicing chords in the key of D.

You'll notice that this sound is identical to the Drop "D" capo. Since you're fingering the two high strings, there's no audible difference between the two chords. But the Short-Cut offers you options. You can remove either of the two fingers on the high strings, and the chord still sounds great.

TRACK 22

Here's a standard D position:

Listen to this D chord with the first string open (you hear an E5):

E5
(D)*

*Similar to D, though not true D chord.

This is the same as a D chord, except you've left the second string open.

E
(D)*

*Similar to D, though not true D chord.

Here you're playing a very simple one-finger chord.

E5
(D)*

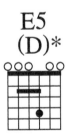

*Similar to D, though not true D chord.

Removing fingers to get different colors from open strings is something that you can continue to do all the way up the neck with different chords. With the Short-Cut capo on the second fret, the rest of the chords in D sound great: Em, F#m, G, A, Bm, and C (the ♭VII chord).

Track 26 demonstrates.

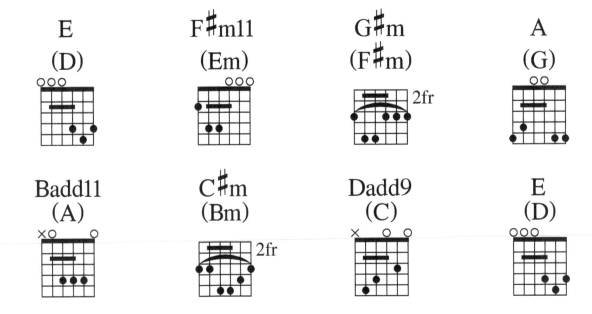

The full chords work just as always; or you can choose to leave some strings open and get some very colorful chords, like this:

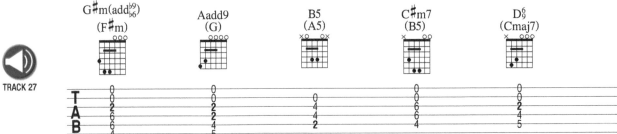

These alternate voicings give you different color options when you play these chords. They all become easier to play—especially the barre chords.

You don't have to change fingerings; in fact, you can play with a Short-Cut just as you would a regular capo, and not change anything at all (except that the Em voicing requires you to play the sixth string on the second fret).

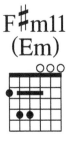

But most often, you don't have to change fingerings at all.

If you're feeling adventurous, try these chords: Dm, F, G, Am, B♭, and C. Listen to *track 29* to hear them.

TRACK 29

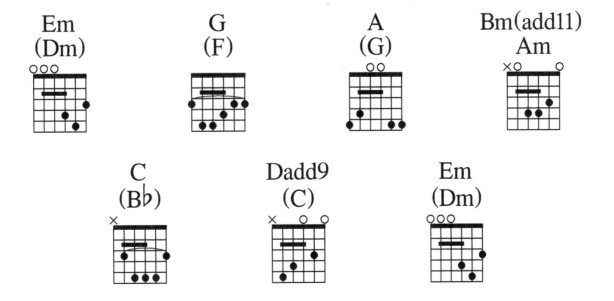

Em
(Dm)

G
(F)

A
(G)

Bm(add11)
Am

C
(B♭)

Dadd9
(C)

Em
(Dm)

C Major

The Short-Cut capo makes it easy for total beginners to learn to play several chords in just minutes. An easy method for teaching complete beginners to play a few chords is by placing the capo on the fourth fret, fingering just one voicing—a Cmaj7 shape that moves up and down the strings.

TRACK 30

Here's the basic Cmaj7 shape. You hear E.

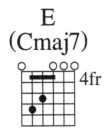

E
(Cmaj7)

4fr

TRACK 31

This is like an F chord shape, except you don't need to barre the high strings. You hear Aadd9/E.

Aadd9/E (F)*

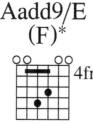
4fr

*Similar to F, though not true F chord.

TRACK 32

This is just like a G chord shape, except you don't need to fret the high strings. You hear Badd11.

Badd11 (G)*

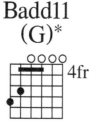
4fr

*Similar to G, though not true G chord.

The basic progression you're playing is C–F–G, and uses only one chord shape. You can play those chords normally, or you can play these simplified chord shapes with a partial capo and get some really unique sounds. And remember, you're still hearing the key of E.

Let's continue following our roadmap. Here are a few more chords in the key of C with the Short-Cut capo on the fourth fret:

TRACK 33

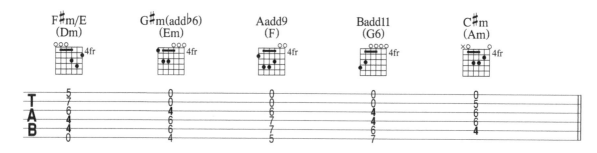

Notice that this F chord is different from the one we just saw. You can play the F however you like; because the open strings sound so good, the Short-Cut gives you options. Same goes for the C and the G. You can take fingers off at will to get new and unique sounds.

Turn It Over

Remember how we said that in standard position, the Short-Cut is **one structural decision** and **two color decisions**? Well, if we turn the capo over, it leaves the high E string open, and the two low strings open. Now we have **two structural decisions** and **one color decision**.

TRACK 34

This doesn't work well in all positions, but here it does. The F chord becomes really easy to play. You hear a nice, full A chord. If you lift your first finger though, you hear a very colorful Aadd#11. Listen to *track 34* to hear that.

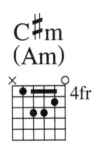

A
(F)

TRACK 35

The Am requires a stretch. You hear C#m.

C#m
(Am)
4fr

This inverted capo will work in a few other positions too. The ninth fret voicing G works well.

Try these chords:

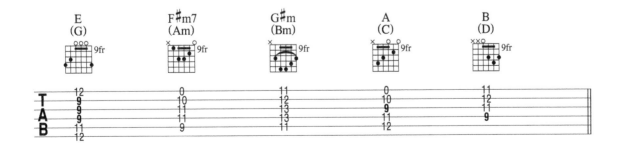

| E (G) | F#m7 (Am) | G#m (Bm) | A (C) | B (D) |

B or B Minor

Let's flip the capo over again to the standard position and play in some other keys. From playing in C on the fourth fret, we move up to the fifth fret and play in B.

The key of B is usually a bear for guitarists—lots of strings to finger, and lots of barre chords.

You may have already noticed that our partial capo roadmap isn't as constrictive as you might think. For example, you can easily play in B or B minor. You can play in other related keys, too. We'll get to that in a bit.

B minor is a bit more forgiving than B major. I'm leaving the diminished ii chord out of this list. If you really miss that sound and absolutely have to play it, odds are pretty good that you know how to create it yourself.

Here are some other chords:

TRACK 36

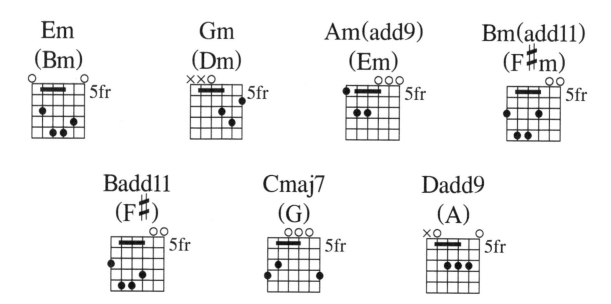

Minor Keys

For the most part, minor keys share notes with their relative major key counterparts (compare A minor and C major, for example). Instead of the diminished seven (vii°) chord, you now have a diminished two (ii°) chord.

But minor keys borrow notes too. In minor keys, the five chords can be minor (v) or major (V)—both are listed above.

A or A Minor

We now move the capo up to the seventh fret and drop our chords down to voicings in the key of A major or A minor. A minor is more approachable, so let's start there.

TRACK 37

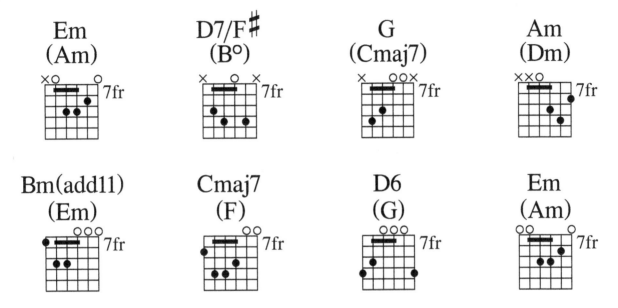

Playing Behind the Capo

With three strings open, it's really easy to play behind the capo, especially if you remember the color/structure distinction. The chord on the right looks like a G chord— and it is! Remember that with the Short-Cut on the seventh fret playing Am, we're actually hearing Em. G is the ♭III chord in the key of Em. So it works. It also works just fine to slide that chord up two frets.

Track 38 demonstrates a groove with the following chords:

TRACK 38

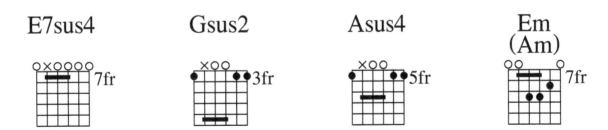

The key of A major works fine here, too. Try A, Bm, C♯m, D, E, F♯m, and G. *Track 39* demonstrates. Some of these barre chords work great by lifting the barres to let the open strings ring.

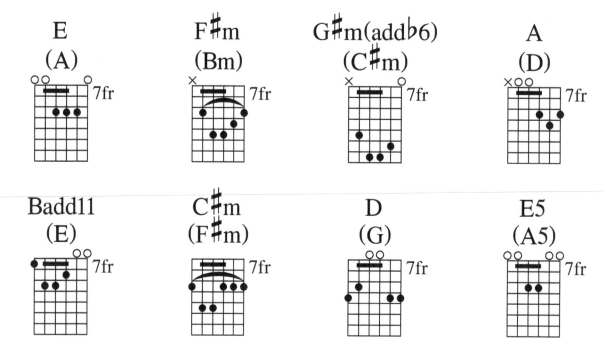

We'll talk more about playing behind the capo on the next page, when we move the capo up two more frets.

G Major

The capo on the ninth fret lends itself well to voicing chords in the key of G major. If your guitar gives you the space to finger chords up here, this position has a very unique sound. The chords you finger high up the neck will be very bright-sounding and almost an octave higher than normal.

But if you take advantage of the drone strings, you also have lower notes to fill out the chord so it doesn't sound tinny. You get a very broad depth of field: low sounds and high sounds.

You hear low notes at the nut, some notes clamped at the ninth fret, and some notes played even higher above it. The effect is almost as if you were playing a piano with your hands spread out wide to the extreme treble and bass keys, then putting your nose down in the middle.

Track 40 demonstrates an example of the lush sounds that are possible: an Emaj9, as shown in the diagram below.

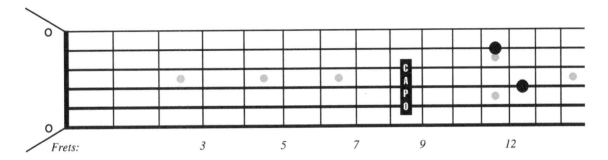

Frets: 3   5   7   9   12

There are lots of great possibilities. Check out these chords:

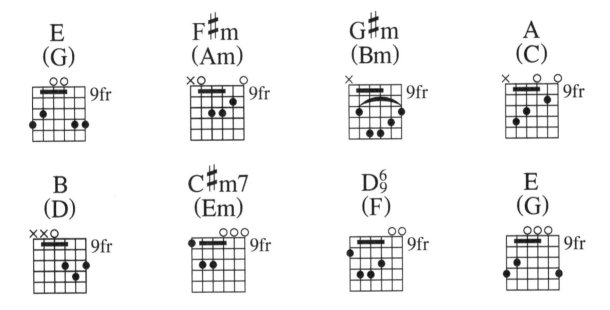

E
(G)
9fr

F#m
(Am)
9fr

G#m
(Bm)
9fr

A
(C)
9fr

B
(D)
9fr

C#m7
(Em)
9fr

D$_9^6$
(F)
9fr

E
(G)
9fr

There's lots of room now to play behind the capo. We'll look at those chords in a minute. First, let's look at thinking structurally, using numbers instead of chord names.

Thinking in Numbers

The next step on the road to transposition is learning to look at chords in terms of **function**. This system of *thinking in numbers* is a great help when working with other musicians who are playing in different keys, too. Let's get started.

G Major Scale

Notes:	G	A	B	C	D	E	F#	G
Scale Tones:	1	2	3	4	5	6	7	1

That's the G major scale. It's nothing to be afraid of—just a series of eight notes from G to G, with a sharp on the seventh note. Think of the first note as "1," the second note as "2," and so on—all the way up to "8," which is actually the same note we started with in a higher octave.

That's almost all there is to thinking in numbers. To make chords, we just put more notes on top of the ones already there, like this:

G Major Scale

Again, that's nothing to be afraid of. All we did was put two more notes above each of the notes of the scale. What we got was three major chords, three minor chords, and a diminished chord. Don't worry about the diminished chord now. Odds are pretty good that you won't play it much. Here's the thing to remember:

In a major key, I, IV, and V are major. Everything else is minor except vii°, which is diminished.

So that's the theory; here's how it works in practice. Take a look at the following chart.

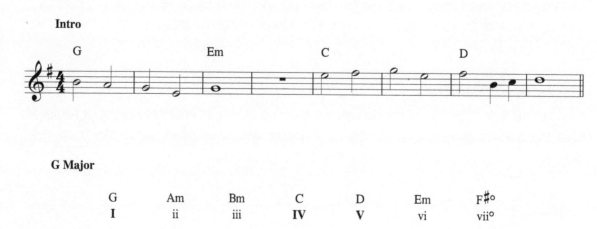

If the chords of a song are G–Em–C–D, that progression is I–vi–IV–V. ("One–six–four–five"—see the chart above.) This might seem academic now, but stick with it. There's a good reason why we're doing it.

That same I–vi–IV–V progression can be used in any major key. Thinking in terms of chord progressions, instead of just chord names, is the secret to **transposing** to other keys, and part of how to effectively use your capo to get more from the guitar.

> ### *Transposition* **can help you in lots of ways:**
> 1. You can play in keys that fit your voice (or someone else's)
> 2. You can play in keys that might otherwise be very difficult to chord
> 3. You can play along with other instruments
> 4. You can play using chords that are idiomatic for the guitar

Idiomatic is a big word for chords that sound good a certain way on a particular instrument. Much of this partial capo work has to do with figuring out what chords sound good with the partial capo in what positions.

Thinking in numbers is really helpful when working in open tunings — and it's about to come in handy now.

Transposing

It's time to apply what we just learned about thinking in numbers. Here's our guitar neck again, with the Short-Cut still on the ninth fret. Strumming the guitar without fingering anything, we more or less have a I chord. It's not exact, but it's close. Playing our chord on the second fret (counted up from the capo, that is), we get a ii chord. On the fourth fret, we have a iii chord, and so on.

Remember that we're still in the key of E, right? Even though our chords above the capo are voiced in the key of G, we're still hearing E. When you're behind the capo, however, you could easily think in E. The open position is E; the ii chord is F#m on the second fret, the iii chord is G#m on the fourth fret, etc. But above the capo, all the voicings look just like the key of G. See the G chord on the twelfth fret down there?

By thinking in numbers, you've resolved the dilemma of thinking in two keys at once.

TRACK 45

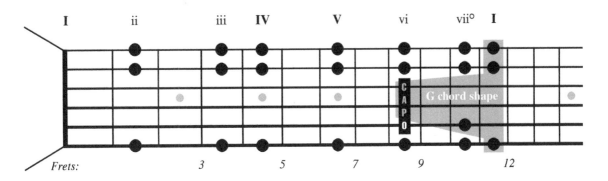

It's important to realize that what we just did is pretty imprecise. You remember the color/structure discussion? By moving the first, second, and sixth strings up, we've changed the structure, but there are still a lot of different colors in there. We made chords that sound okay (some sound more okay than others!), but they're not exactly the same chords.

But for the time being, this approximation is fine. If you don't like how one of these chords sounds, you'll either avoid it, or you'll find ways to add, take away, or change notes to make it work. But notice that by adding a finger on the fifth string, eleventh fret to the twelfth-fret cluster, it looks just like a G chord. The dot on the ninth fret, sixth string is the root of our E minor chord.

Leaving the Road

The roadmap in the first part of this book is just a guide. It's not exact, but it gives enough structure so you can see one way that the partial capo functions (there are more!). If you need to be exact, you certainly can. Lots of guitarists approach open tunings and partial capos by simply letting their fingers find notes that sound good. That approach is fine, if you have the patience to keep at it.

But if you understand why certain things work and certain things don't, you're in much better shape. Let's look at why this roadmap works, then we'll leave the road.

With the Short-Cut capo on the second fret, and nothing fingered, the strings of the guitar sound EBEABE. This is almost an E chord. (It's technically an Esus4.) Because your E chord is already in the strings, you don't have to do much to make consonant sounds, and anything you play in the key of E (you're voicing D, remember!) will sound fine.

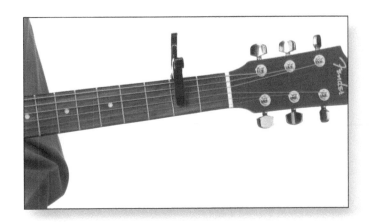

Circle of Fifths

There's one more important piece of music theory that you need to know if you don't already: **the circle of fifths**.

The circle of fifths shows how keys are related to each other. The major keys are on the outside; the relative minor keys are on the inside. At the top is C major. C has no flat notes and no sharp notes—just like A minor. As you go clockwise around the circle, you add one sharp. Going counterclockwise, you add a flat.

With the Short-Cut on the second fret, we're voicing chords in the key of D. Look at the neighboring keys: A and G. If you're going to leave the road, that's a good place to start.

Why? Because the neighboring keys are so closely related that many of the notes are still consonant. If you played in E♭ with the capo in that position, it wouldn't sound so good.

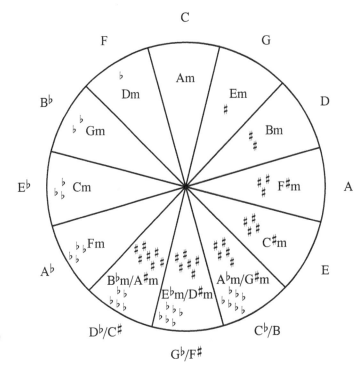

Cross Keys

Now we'll leave the roadmap by venturing out to the neighboring keys. Remember that with the Short-Cut capo on the second fret, we were voicing D major.

D Major/B Minor (capo on 2nd fret)

If you look at the graph, D major and B minor both have two sharps. You can play chords from either of those keys easily, and more often than not, they sound good. You can even play the chords from D minor; they'll work pretty well, too.

If you want to venture further along the circle of fifths, try playing chords in the key of G or Em—or go clockwise around to A or F#m. You can go farther if you like, to C or E— some of those chords work fine, and some are a little harder on the ears.

Remember that the further from the roadmap you go, the more you need to know where you're going in order to make consonant sounds.

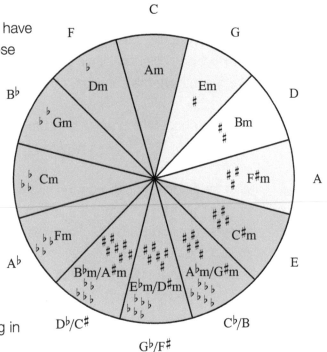

Major Keys

I	ii	iii	IV	V	vi	♭VII	vii°
D	Em	F#m	G	A	Bm	C	C#°
A	Bm	C#m	D	E	F#m	G	G#°
G	Am	Bm	C	D	Em	F	F#°

Minor Keys

i	ii°	♭III	iv	v/V	♭VI	♭VII
Dm	E°	F	Gm	Am/A	B♭	C
Bm	C#°	D	Em	F#m/F#	G	A
Em	F#°	G	Am	Bm/B	C	D
F#m	G#°	A	Bm	C#m/C#	D	E

C Major/A Minor (capo on 4th fret)

Remember that on the fourth fret we were thinking in C major? We can leave the roadmap the same way, by moving around the circle of fifths: up to G/Em, or down to F/Dm.

Some of these chords sound more consonant than others. Keep what you like, and enjoy the process of finding new colors and shapes that sound good to you.

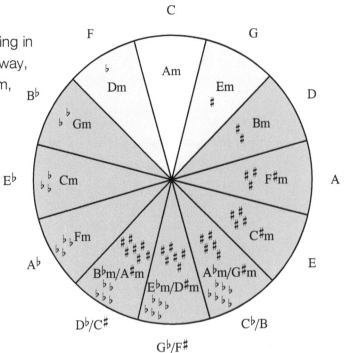

Major Keys

I	ii	iii	IV	V	vi	♭VII	vii°
C	Dm	Em	F	G	Am	B♭	B°
G	Am	Bm	C	D	Em	F	F♯°
F	Gm	Am	B♭	C	Dm	E♭	E°

Minor Keys

i	ii°	♭III	iv	v/V	♭VI	♭VII
Cm	D°	E♭	Fm	Gm/G	A♭	B♭
Am	B°	C	Dm	Em/E	F	G
Em	F♯°	G	Am	Bm/B	C	D
Dm	E°	F	Gm	Am/A	B♭	C

6th fret capo?

As we've written out our roadmap, we haven't dealt with the sixth fret at all. According to the "move capo up, move chord voicing down to stay in E" principle, we'd be playing in B♭ major. B♭ major is a funny key to finger, but the relative minor, G minor, works very well in this position. Try playing behind the capo, too!

A Major/F♯ Minor (capo on 7th fret)

On the seventh fret, the original roadmap key was A. We've already looked at A minor. A major works just fine, as do D and E.

When you choose a key to voice, there are two structural questions to answer: what chord voicings sound good, and where are the drones?

If you choose to voice the key of E, you're stuck fingering the low E string on fret 7 (the same fret as the capo). The A chord (the IV) that you play will have a nice deep bass note to it, whereas the B chord you voice probably won't have those drones. That might be fine if the tune you're playing relies heavily on the IV chord. But what if it doesn't, and you need a full V chord instead? One option is to voice chords in the key of D. The A chord with that nice deep note is now the V chord.

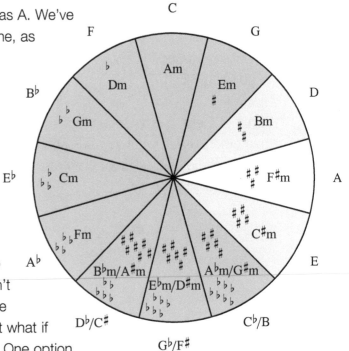

Major Keys

I	ii	iii	IV	V	vi	♭VII	vii°
A	Bm	C♯m	D	E	F♯m	G	G♯°
E	F♯m	G♯m	A	B	C♯m	D	D♯°
D	Em	F♯m	G	A	Bm	C	C♯°

Minor Keys

i	ii°	♭III	iv	v/V	♭VI	♭VII
Am	B°	C	Dm	Em/E	F	G
F♯m	G♯°	A	Bm	C♯m/C♯	D	E
C♯m	D♯°	E	F♯m	G♯m/G♯	A	B
Bm	C♯°	D	Em	F♯m/F♯	G	A

G Major/E Minor (capo on 9th fret)

There's one more cross-key fret to look at: the ninth. Here we were thinking in G. Moving to either side, we go up to D/Bm, or down to C/Am.

The ninth fret is ridiculously high to capo if you're not aiming for a mandolin effect. But as we discussed on page 23, you're not limited to the few remaining frets above the capo.

Once you decide what key you want to play in (C works well here), then you can also look at which chords work well behind the capo and why. Voicing C means that you're actually hearing A. When you bar the fifth fret (with the Short-Cut capo still on fret 9!), you're hearing a I chord variant. Moving up to the seventh fret is your ii chord variant, etc. Barring fret 2 gives you a vi chord variant, and open you've got a V chord variant. Experiment to find what you like!

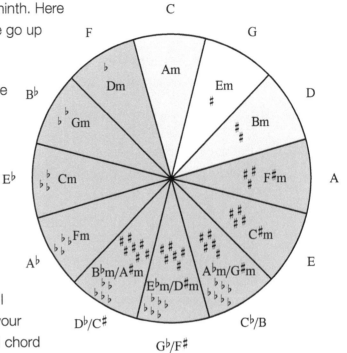

Major Keys

I	ii	iii	IV	V	vi	♭VII	vii°
G	Am	Bm	**C**	**D**	Em	**F**	F#°
D	Em	F#m	**G**	**A**	Bm	**C**	C#°
C	Dm	Em	**F**	**G**	Am	**B♭**	B°

Minor Keys

i	ii°	♭III	iv	v/V	♭VI	♭VII
Gm	A°	**B♭**	Cm	Dm/**D**	**E♭**	**F**
Em	F#°	**G**	Am	Bm/**B**	**C**	**D**
Bm	C#°	**D**	Em	F#m/**F#**	**G**	**A**
Am	B°	**C**	Dm	Em/**E**	**F**	**G**

Cross keys are just one step off the roadmap. We're about to go even further—into the world of multiple capos.

The Next Step: Multiple Capos

Using multiple capos really isn't as scary as it sounds. The easiest way to approach it is through the cross keys that we discussed before.

Two Capos

In the position shown here (Drop "D" capo on fret 2, Short-Cut on fret 4), the C chord works well because of the bass drone. The D chord also works well because of the two high strings. (There's a much deeper theoretical explanation for this, but for the time being we'll leave it at that.) Playing in the key of G uses both the C and D chords, so it's a good place to start.

sixth string is left open

Here's what's formed with the capos alone before you fret any notes:

TRACK 46

Voicing in the key of G works well here. Check out these chords, which will sound in the key of B:

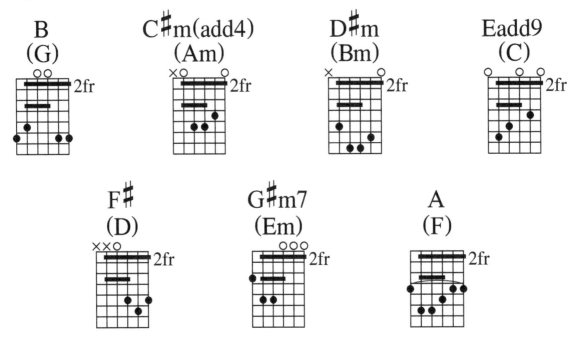

The roadmap works the same way here as it did for the simpler capo work. As you move the Short-Cut capo up, you move down with your chord voicings.

From the previous position, move the Short-Cut up two frets to the sixth fret. Because we were playing in G before, we now move down to F.

Here's what's formed with the capos alone before you fret any notes:

TRACK 47

Check out these chords, voiced in F but still sounding in B:

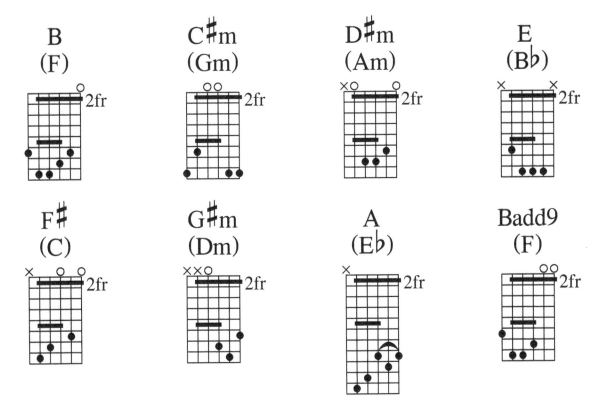

These chords are basic versions of what you can play. For example, the B♭ chord works great if you lift up the barre so that you can hear the open strings ring on the second fret. Also, the ♭VII chord (E♭) is a little awkward—but, remember, these are just suggestions!

You can keep going even further this way if you like; move the Short-Cut up to fret 7 and play in E, or up to fret 9 and play D. The roadmap still works.

Three Capos?

Yes, three capos. On page 6, we had a little talk about the two things a capo does. It helps you change **pitch** or **voicing**. In this picture, the full capo on the first fret is changing the pitch, moving everything up one half step. The other two capos are there to add texture to the voicing you're playing—in this case G major.

sixth string left open for these capos

It almost goes without saying that one full capo works just fine with any partial capo configuration. On any of the partial capo examples in this book, you can add a full capo to raise the pitch.

Here's the example from page 23: the Short-Cut capo on the seventh fret voicing Am. But now we've moved everything up a whole step with a full capo on fret 2 and the Short-Cut on fret 9. Before, we were hearing Em; now we're hearing F#m.

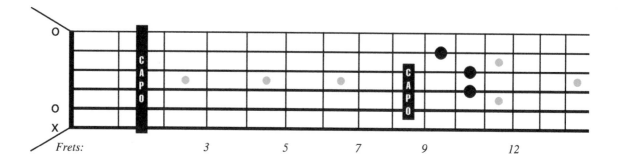

We're about to apply the same theory to open tunings, and it works exactly the same way. Buckle up—the road's about to get bumpier!

Alternate Tunings and Partial Capos

The roadmap for working with alternate tunings is exactly the same as we used for standard tuning. As we move the partial capo up, we drop our chord voicings down. As an example, let's look at DADGAD tuning.

DADGAD tuning is almost open D tuning. But with the third string tuned to G instead of F♯, it's like a Dsus4—or a D with a 4th instead of a 3rd. The 3rd is a very influential note in a chord, and without it the chord becomes ambiguous. But we can use this to our advantage. An ambiguous open tuning makes it easier to play in different keys. This versatility also makes for an easy approach to partial capo work.

The roadmap: In DADGAD with no capo, we're thinking in the key of D major. Now put the Short-Cut on the second fret. Since you've gone up two half steps, take the D chord *down* two half steps—to C. Here are some DADGAD chords in the key of C with the Short-Cut capo on fret 2.

DADGAD:

TRACK 48

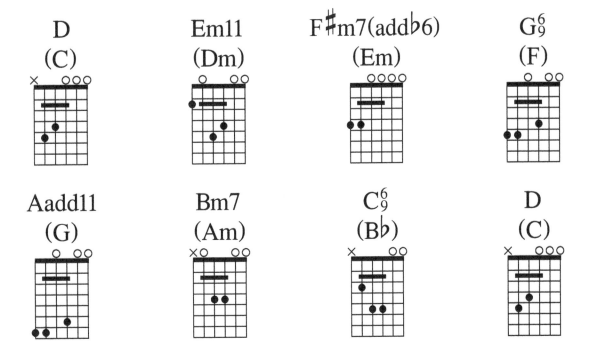

This roadmap will work all the way up the neck. For every fret (or half step) you move the capo up, move your chord voicing down one half step. On the third fret, you can play B or B minor; on the fifth, you can play in the key of A; on the seventh fret you're in G; and on fret 9 you're thinking in F (or D minor). The cross keys are available, too—by moving up or down the circle of fifths.

This approach works for other tunings, too—especially ambiguous ones like DADGAD which don't have a 3rd. Try CGCGCD, for example.

Other Approaches

David Wilcox

David's signature sound is largely due to his open tuning and partial capo work. David often uses a Drop "D" capo on the fifth fret in a G/C tuning (CGDGBD), and also a variation on the same theme in a G/B tuning (BGDGBD) with the capo on the fourth fret. See the chord voicings below — thinking in the key of G, but hearing B.

TRACK 49

BGDGBD:

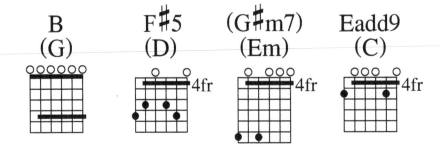

Carrie Newcomer

Carrie began sawing up capos years ago. One of the formations she came up with covers only the D and G strings. She uses it on the second fret, voicing chords in the key of G, or in conjunction with a full capo.

Janis Ian

For years, Janis has used her own modified capo which leaves the first and second strings open, then she tunes to drop D (standard tuning with the low E dropped down to D). It's an effect very similar to the Short-Cut, but not quite the same, because the fingerings change to accommodate the drop D.

It would be easy to think of all the capos we've talked about so far as different, but they're really not.

All the capo positions we've looked at so far are actually very similar. Remember how we talked about color and structure? With high strings open, we made choices that impacted the **color** of a chord, and with low strings open we made choices that impacted the **structure**.

The capo diagrams below are all variations on that same theme of removing outside strings to add color or structure. There are more variations, but these are enough to serve as examples.

Structurally speaking, all of these capos are basically identical. The roadmap we've used so far works for every single one of them.

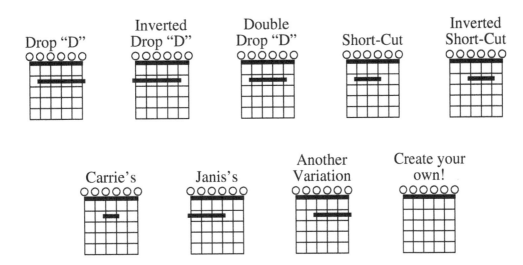

The roadmap laid out in this book is one approach to partial capo work. All of the capos above fall more or less neatly into that "raise capo up, move chord voicing down" pattern, and are easily classified through color and structure.

Harvey Reid: The Third Hand Capo

Harvey's probably the reason why partial capos are used at all. In 1976 Harvey began experimenting with capoing only a few strings on the guitar. Around the same time, an inventor in California named Lyle Shabram was trying to sell his "Chord-Forming capo." Lyle's idea was that the capo would form a chord or part of a chord to facilitate playing. He was right, though at the time, he didn't know how right he was.

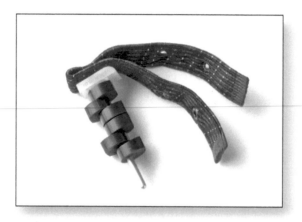

The two men were doing similar experiments, unaware of each other. Lyle took out an ad for his capo in a guitar magazine, and that's when Harvey found him.

Lyle licensed the patent for his device. Harvey Reid and Jeff Hickey formed the Third Hand Capo Company and began selling Third Hand capos in stores in 1980.

One Open String

The Third Hand capos are great for experimentation, because you can choose exactly which strings you want to capo. You can even use several Third Hands at once the same way we used the Short-Cut and the Drop "D" together. So far, we've dealt with capos which clamp inside strings and let outside strings ring. The Short-Cut and Drop "D" and their variations all fit into that category.

Another approach is to remove *inside* strings while clamping outside strings. Lots of folks saw up their capos for this, or use a Third Hand that was built for this purpose.

Some guitarists remove one of the inside strings and leave the others clamped, in standard or open tunings. Some leave two inside strings open; others leave three or more. Both "Woody's G-Band" capos are extreme examples of this, clamping only one or two outside strings.

An example of one open string is a staple of Harvey Reid's repertoire: playing in an open major tuning and capoing on the first fret, leaving the third degree of the scale open. This sounds like an open minor tuning, but allows for barres to be played that form major chords.

Perhaps a more approachable way to leave one string open is in standard tuning, using the open string as a color note. Try this open 9th (sus2) form, for example:

Fsus2
(Em)

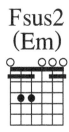

Here you're playing Em, but because of the barre and open string, you hear Fsus2. (The open G string is the 2nd, or 9th, of the chord.)

TRACK 50

Try this simple progression, voicing the key of Em:

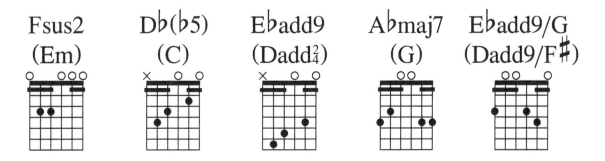

| Fsus2 (Em) | Db(b5) (C) | Ebadd9 (Dadd$\frac{2}{4}$) | Abmaj7 (G) | Ebadd9/G (Dadd9/F♯) |

The roadmap (moving the capo up while moving the chord voicings down) works just fine here. On the first fret you played Em. Therefore when you capo on the third you play Dm, and on the fifth, Cm if you're so inclined. Continue on to Bm on the sixth, Am on the eighth, etc. There's plenty of room for exploration, depending on which string you leave open.

Try another approach to the same open 9th idea, this time leaving the B string open.

Am9
(Em)

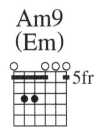

5fr

Here's the same progression with the capo on the fifth fret (so it sounds in Am); the same 9th is ringing:

TRACK 51

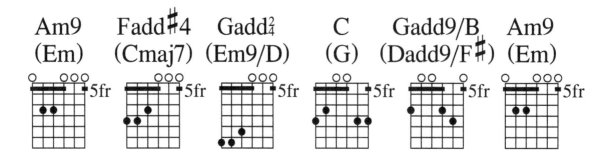

Am9	Fadd#4	Gadd$\frac{2}{4}$	C	Gadd9/B	Am9
(Em)	(Cmaj7)	(Em9/D)	(G)	(Dadd9/F#)	(Em)

The roadmap applies here, too. From Em on fret 5, you have Dm on the seventh fret, etc. Going down works too, although there are other reasons why that's problematic.

Three Open Strings

Chris Monaghan developed what he calls "the open capo method," in which he uses a modified Kyser six-string capo with the third, fourth, and fifth strings cut out (the opposite of the Short-Cut).

The roadmap in this book involves changing voicings but staying in the same key (E major). Chris's system keeps the same voicing (key of E major) but moves the capo to change the key. Above the capo, all the chords are voicings in the key of E major. Below the capo, the voicings are whatever key you're playing in at that moment.

These voicings in the key of G work behind the capo. Notice how in the G chord most of the strings are already fretted for you on the third fret. These chords are also available above the capo, but then you'd be voicing the key of E major.

TRACK 52

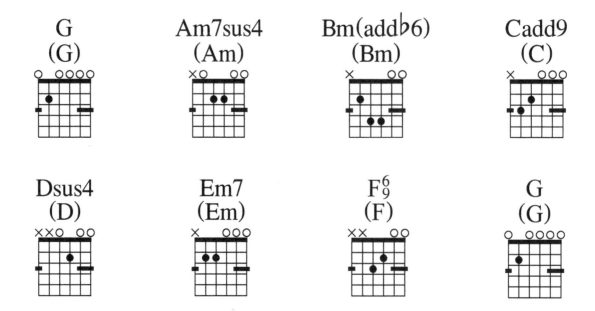

G	Am7sus4	Bm(add♭6)	Cadd9
(G)	(Am)	(Bm)	(C)

Dsus4	Em7	F$^6_9$	G
(D)	(Em)	(F)	(G)

Notice how these voicings mostly cover the open strings, and for the most part look like standard barre chords without the full barres.

TRACK 53

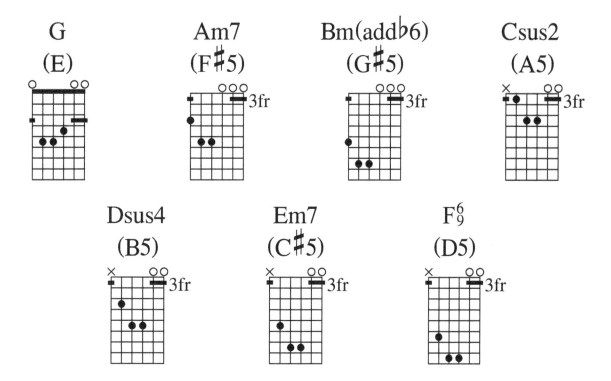

One Last Thing

This may seem a little far-fetched, but here's what songwriter Bill Nash is up to these days. Bill wrote a song using *four* capos. He's not just being goofy; Bill has limited use of his hands, and the unique sounds he gets from using partial capos give him lots of possibilities with just one- and two-fingered chords.

TRACK 54

This guitar is in DADGAD, and these capos give the guitar a haunting E♭m9 sound.

This may seem complicated, but the partial capo is only thirty years old. Who knows what we'll find in another thirty years?

I also suspect that there's more to be found from analyzing this position in depth.

CONCLUSION

Lots of folks have contributed to my understanding of partial capo work, and I'm grateful to them all: Harvey Reid, David Wilcox, Johnsmith, Bill Isles, Willy Porter, Cosy Sheridan, Don Conoscenti, Carrie Newcomer, Chris Monaghan, Trace Bundy, and especially Justin Roth for his insight about cross keys and open tunings.

There's lots of information in this book. Hopefully you've found it helpful to understanding more about how to use capos, and you feel reasonably confident with the new skills you've learned. Thanks for sticking with it. If you find anything interesting, please do drop me a line.

- Randall Williams
(randall@whereisrandall.com)

AUDIO TRACK LIST

Get Better at Guitar

...with these Great Guitar Instruction Books from Hal Leonard!

101 GUITAR TIPS
STUFF ALL THE PROS KNOW AND USE
by Adam St. James
This book contains invaluable guidance on everything from scales and music theory to truss rod adjustments, proper recording studio set-ups, and much more.
00695737 Book/Online Audio $17.99

AMAZING PHRASING
by Tom Kolb
This book/audio pack explores all the main components necessary for crafting well-balanced rhythmic and melodic phrases. It also explains how these phrases are put together to form cohesive solos. The companion audio contains 89 demo tracks, most with full-band backing.
00695583 Book/Online Audio $22.99

ARPEGGIOS FOR THE MODERN GUITARIST
by Tom Kolb
Using this no-nonsense book with online audio, guitarists will learn to apply and execute all types of arpeggio forms using a variety of techniques, including alternate picking, sweep picking, tapping, string skipping, and legato.
00695862 Book/Online Audio $22.99

BLUES YOU CAN USE
by John Ganapes
This comprehensive source for learning blues guitar is designed to develop both your lead and rhythm playing. Includes: 21 complete solos • blues chords, progressions and riffs • turnarounds • movable scales and soloing techniques • string bending • utilizing the entire fingerboard • and more.
00142420 Book/Online Media...................................$22.99

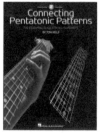

CONNECTING PENTATONIC PATTERNS
by Tom Kolb
If you've been finding yourself trapped in the pentatonic box, this book is for you! This hands-on book with online audio offers examples for guitar players of all levels, from beginner to advanced. Study this book faithfully, and soon you'll be soloing all over the neck with the greatest of ease.
00696445 Book/Online Audio $24.99

FRETBOARD MASTERY
by Troy Stetina
Untangle the mysterious regions of the guitar fretboard and unlock your potential. This book familiarizes you with all the shapes you need to know by applying them in real musical examples, thereby reinforcing and reaffirming your newfound knowledge.
00695331 Book/Online Audio $22.99

GUITAR AEROBICS
by Troy Nelson
Here is a daily dose of guitar "vitamins" to keep your chops fine tuned! Musical styles include rock, blues, jazz, metal, country, and funk. Techniques taught include alternate picking, arpeggios, sweep picking, string skipping, legato, string bending, and rhythm guitar.
00695946 Book/Online Audio $24.99

GUITAR CLUES
OPERATION PENTATONIC
by Greg Koch
Whether you're new to improvising or have been doing it for a while, this book/audio pack will provide loads of delicious licks and tricks that you can use right away, from volume swells and chicken pickin' to intervallic and chordal ideas.
00695827 Book/Online Audio $19.99

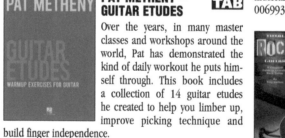

PAT METHENY – GUITAR ETUDES
Over the years, in many master classes and workshops around the world, Pat has demonstrated the kind of daily workout he puts himself through. This book includes a collection of 14 guitar etudes he created to help you limber up, improve picking technique and build finger independence.
00696587...$17.99

PICTURE CHORD ENCYCLOPEDIA
This comprehensive guitar chord resource for all playing styles and levels features five voicings of 44 chord qualities for all twelve keys – 2,640 chords in all! For each, there is a clearly illustrated chord frame, as well as *an actual photo* of the chord being played!.
00695224...$22.99

RHYTHM GUITAR 365
by Troy Nelson
This book provides 365 exercises – one for every day of the year! – to keep your rhythm chops fine tuned. Topics covered include: chord theory; the fundamentals of rhythm; fingerpicking; strum patterns; diatonic and non-diatonic progressions; triads; major and minor keys; and more.
00103627 Book/Online Audio $27.99

SCALE CHORD RELATIONSHIPS
by Michael Mueller & Jeff Schroedl
This book/audio pack explains how to: recognize keys • analyze chord progressions • use the modes • play over nondiatonic harmony • use harmonic and melodic minor scales • use symmetrical scales • incorporate exotic scales • and much more!
00695563 Book/Online Audio $17.99

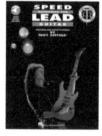

SPEED MECHANICS FOR LEAD GUITAR
by Troy Stetina
Take your playing to the stratosphere with this advanced lead book which will help you develop speed and precision in today's explosive playing styles. Learn the fastest ways to achieve speed and control, secrets to make your practice time really count, and how to open your ears and make your musical ideas more solid and tangible.
00699323 Book/Online Audio $22.99

TOTAL ROCK GUITAR
by Troy Stetina
This comprehensive source for learning rock guitar is designed to develop both lead and rhythm playing. It covers: getting a tone that rocks • open chords, power chords and barre chords • riffs, scales and licks • string bending, strumming, and harmonics • and more.
00695246 Book/Online Audio $22.99

Guitar World Presents STEVE VAI'S GUITAR WORKOUT
In this book, Steve Vai reveals his path to virtuoso enlightenment with two challenging guitar workouts – one 10-hour and one 30-hour – which include scale and chord exercises, ear training, sight-reading, music theory, and much more.
00119643...$16.99

INCLUDES TAB

EXPAND YOUR ACOUSTIC GUITAR KNOWLEDGE

ACOUSTIC GUITAR CHORDS
INCLUDES TAB DVD

by Chad Johnson

In any music style, there are essentials – scales, licks, chords, etc. This book teaches you the must-know chords that will get you strumming quickly. Rather, you'll be armed with many chord shapes that have been used throughout the acoustic guitar's history in countless hits. The included DVD demonstrates each chord and all the examples are accompanied by a full band.

00696484 Book/DVD Pack............................$9.99

ACOUSTIC GUITAR LESSON PACK
INCLUDES TAB DVD

This boxed set includes four books (*Acoustic Guitar Method*, *Guitar Chord Chart*, *Guitar Scale Chart*, and *Guitar Theory*) and the *200 Acoustic Licks* DVD that includes tasty lead lines and fingerstyle phrases, creative riffs, walk-through explanations by pro guitarists, note-for-note on-screen tablature; normal- and slow-speed performance demos.

00131554 4 Books & 1 DVD........................$29.99

FIRST 15 LESSONS – ACOUSTIC GUITAR
INCLUDES TAB

by Troy Nelson

The First 15 Lessons series provides a step-by-step lesson plan for the absolute beginner, complete with audio tracks, video lessons, and real songs! The acoustic guitar book, features lessons on: guitar fundamentals, chords, strumming, arpeggios, time signatures, syncopation, hammer-ons & pull-offs, double stops, harmonics, fingerpicking, alternate picking, and scales & basic theory.

00696484 Book/Online Media.......................$9.99

THE HAL LEONARD ACOUSTIC GUITAR METHOD
INCLUDES TAB

by Chad Johnson

This method uses real songs to teach you all the basics of acoustic guitar in the style of the Beatles, Eric Clapton, John Mellencamp, James Taylor and many others. Lessons include: strumming; fingerpicking; using a capo; open tunings; folk, country & bluegrass styles; acoustic blues; acoustic rock; and more.

00697347 Book/Online Audio......................$17.99

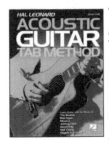

THE HAL LEONARD ACOUSTIC GUITAR TAB METHOD
INCLUDES TAB

Learn chords with songs like "Eleanor Rigby" and "Knockin' on Heaven's Door," single notes with riffs and solos by Nirvana and Pink Floyd, arpeggios with classics by Eric Clapton and Boston, and more. This method's well-paced, logical teaching sequence will get students playing more easily than ever before, and music from popular artists like the Eagles, Johnny Cash & Green Day keeps them playing and having fun.

00124197 Book/Online Audio......................$12.99
00146365 Book Only....................................$6.99

HAL LEONARD FINGERSTYLE GUITAR METHOD
INCLUDES TAB

by Chad Johnson

The *Hal Leonard Fingerstyle Guitar Method* is your complete guide to learning fingerstyle guitar. Songs covered include: Annie's Song • Blowin' in the Wind • Dust in the Wind • Fire and Rain • Georgia on My Mind • Imagine • Landslide • Tears in Heaven • What a Wonderful World • Yesterday • You've Got a Friend • and more.

00697378 Book/Online Audio......................$21.99

HOW TO FINGERPICK SONGS ON GUITAR
INCLUDES TAB

by Chad Johnson

Learn fingerstyle techniques from the ground up with exercises, songs, and videos designed to lead you into a whole new world of guitar enjoyment. Along the way, you will also explore how to create solo-guitar arrangements of your favorite songs using a variety of methods. Plus every technique, topic, playing example, and song in the book is demonstrated for you on video!

00155364 Book/Online Video......................$14.99

100 ACOUSTIC LESSONS
INCLUDES TAB

by Chad Johnson and Michael Mueller

Featuring 100 individual modules covering a giant array of topics, each lesson in this Acoustic volume includes detailed instruction with playing examples presented in standard notation and tablature. You'll also get extremely useful tips, scale diagrams, chord grids, photos, and more to reinforce your learning experience, plus online audio with performance demos of examples in the book!

00696456 Book/Online Audio.....................$24.99

PERCUSSIVE ACOUSTIC GUITAR METHOD
INCLUDES TAB

by Chris Woods

Providing detailed, step-by-step instruction on a variety of percussive guitar techniques, this book includes warm-ups, exercises, full peices, and pracitcal "how-to" training that will get you slapping and tapping. Covers: string slapping, body percussion, tapping, harmonics, alternate tunings, standard notation & tab, and more!

00696643 Book/Online Video.....................$19.99

PLAY ACOUSTIC GUITAR IN MINUTES

by Andrew DuBrock

This fantastic beginner's guide will get your fingers on the fretboard in no time! You'll quickly learn easy chords, basic fingerpicking, strumming patterns, chord progressions, and much more. The online video features over 2 hours of instruction with Andrew DuBrock himself as your personal teacher, reinforcing all the lessons in the book.

00696621 Book/Online Video.....................$21.99

TOTAL ACOUSTIC GUITAR
INCLUDES TAB

by Andrew DuBrock

Packed with tons of examples and audio demonstrations, this book/online audio package breaks down the most common, essential acoustic techniques with clear, concise instruction and then applies them to real-world musical riffs, licks, and songs. You'll learn syncopation, power chords, arpeggios, rhythm fills, and much more.

00696072 Book/Online Audio.....................$19.99

TRAVIS PICKING
INCLUDES TAB

by Andrew DuBrock

From the backwoods of Kentucky to modern-day concert arenas, the Travis picking technique has been a guitar staple for generations. In this guide, you'll go step-by-step from basic accompaniment patterns to advanced fingerpicking methods in the style of Merle, Chet and others.

00696425 Book/Online Audio.....................$16.99

HAL•LEONARD®

www.halleonard.com

*Prices, contents, and availability
subject to change without notice.*

0321

HAL LEONARD GUITAR METHOD

METHOD BOOKS, SONGBOOKS AND REFERENCE BOOKS

THE HAL LEONARD GUITAR METHOD is designed for anyone just learning to play acoustic or electric guitar. It is based on years of teaching guitar students of all ages, and it also reflects some of the best guitar teaching ideas from around the world. This comprehensive method includes: A learning sequence carefully paced with clear instructions; popular songs which increase the incentive to learn to play; versatility – can be used as self-instruction or with a teacher; audio accompaniments so that students have fun and sound great while practicing.

BOOK 1
00699010	Book Only	$8.99
00699027	Book/Online Audio	$12.99
00697341	Book/Online Audio + DVD	$24.99
00697318	DVD Only	$19.99
00155480	Deluxe Beginner Edition (Book, CD, DVD, Online Audio/Video & Chord Poster)	$19.99

COMPLETE (BOOKS 1, 2 & 3)
00699040	Book Only	$16.99
00697342	Book/Online Audio	$24.99

BOOK 2
00699020	Book Only	$8.99
00697313	Book/Online Audio	$12.99

BOOK 3
00699030	Book Only	$8.99
00697316	Book/Online Audio	$12.99

Prices, contents and availability subject to change without notice.

STYLISTIC METHODS

ACOUSTIC GUITAR
00697347	Method Book/Online Audio	$17.99
00237969	Songbook/Online Audio	$16.99

BLUEGRASS GUITAR
00697405	Method Book/Online Audio	$16.99

BLUES GUITAR
00697326	Method Book/Online Audio (9" x 12")	$16.99
00697344	Method Book/Online Audio (6" x 9")	$15.99
00697385	Songbook/Online Audio (9" x 12")	$14.99
00248636	Kids Method Book/Online Audio	$12.99

BRAZILIAN GUITAR
00697415	Method Book/Online Audio	$17.99

CHRISTIAN GUITAR
00695947	Method Book/Online Audio	$16.99
00697408	Songbook/CD Pack	$14.99

CLASSICAL GUITAR
00697376	Method Book/Online Audio	$15.99

COUNTRY GUITAR
00697337	Method Book/Online Audio	$22.99
00697400	Songbook/Online Audio	$19.99

FINGERSTYLE GUITAR
00697378	Method Book/Online Audio	$21.99
00697432	Songbook/Online Audio	$16.99

FLAMENCO GUITAR
00697363	Method Book/Online Audio	$15.99

FOLK GUITAR
00697414	Method Book/Online Audio	$16.99

JAZZ GUITAR
00695359	Book/Online Audio	$22.99
00697386	Songbook/Online Audio	$15.99

JAZZ-ROCK FUSION
00697387	Book/Online Audio	$24.99

R&B GUITAR
00697356	Book/Online Audio	$19.99
00697433	Songbook/CD Pack	$14.99

ROCK GUITAR
00697319	Book/Online Audio	$16.99
00697383	Songbook/Online Audio	$16.99

ROCKABILLY GUITAR
00697407	Book/Online Audio	$16.99

OTHER METHOD BOOKS

BARITONE GUITAR METHOD
00242055	Book/Online Audio	$12.99

GUITAR FOR KIDS
00865003	Method Book 1/Online Audio	$12.99
00697402	Songbook/Online Audio	$9.99
00128437	Method Book 2/Online Audio	$12.99

MUSIC THEORY FOR GUITARISTS
00695790	Book/Online Audio	$19.99

TENOR GUITAR METHOD
00148330	Book/Online Audio	$12.99

12-STRING GUITAR METHOD
00249528	Book/Online Audio	$19.99

METHOD SUPPLEMENTS

ARPEGGIO FINDER
00697352	6" x 9" Edition	$6.99
00697351	9" x 12" Edition	$9.99

BARRE CHORDS
00697406	Book/Online Audio	$14.99

CHORD, SCALE & ARPEGGIO FINDER
00697410	Book Only	$19.99

GUITAR TECHNIQUES
00697389	Book/Online Audio	$16.99

INCREDIBLE CHORD FINDER
00697200	6" x 9" Edition	$7.99
00697208	9" x 12" Edition	$7.99

INCREDIBLE SCALE FINDER
00695568	6" x 9" Edition	$9.99
00695490	9" x 12" Edition	$9.99

LEAD LICKS
00697345	Book/Online Audio	$10.99

RHYTHM RIFFS
00697346	Book/Online Audio	$14.99

SONGBOOKS

CLASSICAL GUITAR PIECES
00697388	Book/Online Audio	$9.99

EASY POP MELODIES
00697281	Book Only	$7.99
00697440	Book/Online Audio	$14.99

(MORE) EASY POP MELODIES
00697280	Book Only	$6.99
00697269	Book/Online Audio	$14.99

(EVEN MORE) EASY POP MELODIES
00699154	Book Only	$6.99
00697439	Book/Online Audio	$14.99

EASY POP RHYTHMS
00697336	Book Only	$7.99
00697441	Book/Online Audio	$14.99

(MORE) EASY POP RHYTHMS
00697338	Book Only	$7.99
00697322	Book/Online Audio	$14.99

(EVEN MORE) EASY POP RHYTHMS
00697340	Book Only	$7.99
00697323	Book/Online Audio	$14.99

EASY POP CHRISTMAS MELODIES
00697417	Book Only	$9.99
00697416	Book/Online Audio	$14.99

EASY POP CHRISTMAS RHYTHMS
00278177	Book Only	$6.99
00278175	Book/Online Audio	$14.99

EASY SOLO GUITAR PIECES
00110407	Book Only	$9.99

REFERENCE

GUITAR PRACTICE PLANNER
00697401	Book Only	$5.99

GUITAR SETUP & MAINTENANCE
00697427	6" x 9" Edition	$14.99
00697421	9" x 12" Edition	$12.99

For more info, songlists, or to purchase these and more books from your favorite music retailer, go to

halleonard.com

HAL•LEONARD®